Reeder McCandless] [from old catalog] [Fish

The Grim Chieftan of Kansas

and other free-state men in their struggles against slavery

Reeder McCandless] [from old catalog] [Fish

The Grim chieftan of Kansas
and other free-state men in their struggles against slavery

ISBN/EAN: 9783744741378

Printed in Europe, USA, Canada, Australia, Japan

Cover: Foto ©ninafisch / pixelio.de

More available books at **www.hansebooks.com**

—THE—
GRIM CHIEFTAIN
of Kansas,

And Other Free-State Men in Their Struggles Against Slavery.

Some Political Seances, Incidents, Inside Political Views and Movements in their Career.

—BY—

One Who Knows.

CHERRYVILE, KANSAS
CLARION BOOK & JOB PRINT
1885.

COPYRIGHT, 1885
By LILLIE K. SHEWARD.
ALL RIGHTS RESERVED.

PUBLISHER'S PREFACE.

A part of this work was published in the Baldwin CRITERION in the winter of 1884-85, and created considerable interest at that time, which is the only excuse we have for putting it out in book form.

Taken as a whole, this work now offered to the public is, we suppose, without question the most graphic and complete presentation of an era altogether the most remarkable in the history of the most important personage (James Lane) known in the early struggles of Kansas which ever has been, or is likely to be written.—

Being written as it is by "one who knows" (since deceased,) having been intimately acquainted with the Grim Cheiftain long before his advent into Kansas and written without bias or motive of any kind.

It is confidently hoped that the thoughtful reader will find a renewed and stronger faith in the value of the work, completed as it is by the serried array of facts and figures and the thrilling recitals of personal experience with which it reveals the scope, methods, and power of that terrible reality. "The Grim Cheiftain in his struggles against slavery."

THE
GRIM CHIEFTAIN
OF KANSAS,

AND OTHER FREE-STATE MEN IN THEIR
STRUGGLES AGAINST SLAVERY.

BY ONE WHO KNOWS.

Your correspondent has often thought that, if he were gifted with the genius and poetic fire of Homer of old or possessed the dramatic talent of Shakespeare or was endowed with the literary ability of a Defoe or a Dumas, he could, provided a sufficient length of time had elapsed from the occurence of the scenes, wish for no better subject, to immortalize his name than the career of this once famous personage of Kansas history and others connected with him Their whole career with those around him, was one continued poem varied by scenes of grandeur and sublimity equaled only by the Grecian Achilles as sung by the father of song: And since truth is stranger than fiction, were these scenes properly written or portrayed, they would almost cause the author of Macbeth or the great masters of romance themselves, though they be now dwellers in the spirit land, to fear for the fate and fame of their works in the world here below. But while nothing of the kind is even thought of, let alone contemplated, yet, your correspondent, looking through terrestial mediums, believes that, there are many things connected with the career of this singular man that never have been made public, and consequently known to but few or himself alone, which will be both interesting and amusing to your readers, many of whom were once his personal and political friends and also his companions and co-workers, during those exciting and turbulent times, which made Kansas a free state. To the people of Baldwin, he was largely indebted for this political success. Their support, which he always professed to prize very highly, gave him a moral prestige, which was of the greatest advantage to him in other localities. One of your citizens, in obedience to the known wishes of your people, at a sacrifice to himself which no man ought to have been called on to make, when there was no other escape possible, saved him from final defeat.

There will be no attempt to write his life or a history of his times. What is common place or well known will not be repeated. To defend, or condemn him, or to write him or any one else, who may have been connected, in any way, with him or his career, "up or down," or to make them white or black, is no part of the present plan or purpose. Like most others who were brought into contact with him, your correspondent has been both his political friend and foe, but at this late day, has no views, nor opinions of his own with regard to him or others of that period, that he cares to uphold; nor, has he any inclination or wish to combat the views of others. He has no friends to reward, and no enemies to punish. He owes no man, save one, anything, and him he never can repay. Besides he is long since out of politics, which, when interpreted into plain language, means that he is politically dead and buried beyond all hope of resurrection, except that as he may be permitted to occasionally return and hold a political seance with his friends through the CRITERION. What he writes will, therefore be without bias or motive of any kind But some however will wish they never had been politicians or that these seances never had been written and that departed spirits from the world of politics or any other world should remain where they belong.

CHAPTER I.

His father. His entry into this mundane sphere. His early training and first public speech. His election to the Legislature. His election as Colonel of volunteers for the Mexican war. His election to Congress.

HIS FATHER

rejoiced in the prophetic and scriptural cognomen of Amos, but nobody ever suspected that the sanctity of this name had any effect upon his life or influence over his conduct. He was a disciple of Blackstone, by profession and a Democratic politician by nature He was one of the three illustrious statesmen who composed the first state convention that ever declared for the hero of New Orleans for president. One of the three was made chairman of the convention, another secretary, when Amos the Father of the Chieftian, drew forth and read the necessary whereases, and resolutions declaring that for president of these

United States Gen. Andrew Jackson of Tennessee, the soldier, patriot and statesman was the unanimous choice of this,the largest and most enthusiastic convention ever assembled in the state of Indiana. Thus the ball was started that rolled old Hickory into the White House.

HIS APPEARANCE ON THIS PLANET.

Whether the Chieftain was "born a baby." the way in which. the great senator from South Carolina in her palmest days of slavery, says that all men came into this world; or whether he was one of the „all men" that the declaration of independence declares were born "free and equal"or whether he entered onto this terrestial sphere in some other way peculiar to himself alone, does not matter. He got here in some way and that was sufficient for his purpose and ours too.

His earliest instructions were in the Democratic faith and his walk therein was blameless, even from his childhood. His early imitations of Demosthenes and Cicero were made in little Democratic speeches, which were prepared or selected by his Democratic mother or father. He claimed to have made

HIS FIRST PUBLIC SPEECH

when he was but thirteen years of age and that it was orthodox, according to the Democratic faith, and was so considered by all who heard it. He continued to make political speeches from that time, as a sort of a Democratic prodigy or nondescript until he was twenty years of age, when he was

ELECTED TO THE LEGISLATURE

of his state, but could not qualify and take his seat until he was twenty-one which occured soon after the meeting of the legislature to which he was elected. He gave very general satisfaction to his party and they continued to elect him until the breaking out of the Mexican war, when not satisfied with persuits of peace nor the honors of his state,

But longed for deeds of war and glory;

He then sought the position of colonel of one of the regiments of volunteers which his state was then raising for service in the Mexican war. He had several competitors for the place and the contest was very bitter. Among other things his enemies, as he always called his political opponents, charged him with killing three men. And this charge, which was considered the most likely to insure his defeat, was pressed against him with the utmost pertinacity. To the utter astonishment of his friends and every body else, he made no denial or explanation of it, nor replied to it in any way whatever. And when any of his friends would speak to him about it, he would simply say "Never mind, that's all right. That's what,s going to elect me."

When the day for the election of field officers came, he made a speech to the men, and at the conclusion, looking as solemn as we may imagine Lazarus to have looked when he came forth out of his sepulchre with his grave clothes on said: "My enemies say that I have killed three men. What do men go to war for? Is it not to kill men? Now, if I have killed three men, as they say I have, in time of peace, when there was no war, am I not for that reason a fit man to lead you to war where you are going to kill men? Am I not, on that account the very best man you could have to lead you to war?" It is scarcely necessary to say that the men looked on or saw it in that light. He was triumphantly elected and soon after departed with his brave regiment for the crimson fields of deadly strife where glory and fame was awaiting him in the land of the Montezumas and Aztecs—and his men never regretted that they had chosen him to lead them to war.

HIS ELECTION TO CONGRESS.

Not long after his return from the Mexican war, the Chieftain appears as a candidate for a seat in the congress of the United States. As usual his enemies were plentiful and among many other things, the editor of a leading paper charged and proved that he had promised to procure appointments for twenty-three men in the district for their support, if he was elected. To deny the charge in the face of the proof, it was thought would work his political ruin, and to admit or evade them would be equally disastrous, if not more so. Let him take whichever horn of the dilemma he chose, the editor thought that he was in a position to say: "I have met the enemy and he is mine."

Having read the article carefully through, the Chieftian stretching forth the hand in which he held the paper, and running his long fingers of the other hand through the hair on the side of his forehead, said, in a sort of a yawning way, to the friends who handed him the paper and were watching to see what effect it would have on him, "That's all right. That article elects me, sure." "How is that," said some one. "I tell you it is so. Come to the meeting to night and you will see."

THE MEETING.

There was a grand rally of the Democracy that night, with many of the opposition, who expected to see the Chieftain flay the editor alive and disprove or deny that he had ever made any such promises.

SYNOPSIS OF HIS SPEECH.

His speech that night was in his best and happiest style, and may be said to be one of the greatest, if not the greatest effort of his whole life. He declared.

"That the institution of 'nigger' slavery was of Divine origin and appointment and was instituted for the best good, of both the 'nigger' (this is the way he wrotte his word then,) and the white races. That the 'nigger' while they possessed great physical powers, and were well adapted to labor in warm and malarial climates were mentally inferior and without capacity for improvement, and needed the intelligence and skill of the superior white race to superintend their labor so as to conduce in the best manner to their subsistance. Thus, the best interest of both races, was subserved and the wisdom of the Divine economy made manifest. That the condition of the 'niggers' in slavery in the southern states was vastly superior to the condition of those in Africa where they had not the benefit of the intelligence of white men to direct them

"That the institution of human slavery was in accord with the plainest teachings of the Bible. Was not Ham cursed. Most assuredly he was. 'Cursed be Canaan, a servant of servants shall he be unto his brethern.' 'Servants obey your master.' 'Servants be obedient unto your masters.' That the constitution of our country recognizes and sanctions it. This the abolitionists, themselves allow when they declare that the constitution of the United States is a league with death and a covenant with hell. That the fugitive slave law was in strict accordance with the constitution, which provides in plain language that person who owe service or labor and should escape into another state, should be given up to the persons to whom such labor or service was due. Did not Paul return Onesimus, who was a fugitive slave, to Philemon, his master? That slaves were made property by the constitution, the same as horses or mules and their masters or owners had the same moral and legal right to reclaim a fugitive slave, that they had to retake an estray mule or horse. That the abolitionists were worse than infidels, for they ignore the plainest teachings of the Bible in which they profess to believe. That they deserved not only the maledictions execrations and anathemas of all good citizens, but also the severest punishment for their crimes against the constitution and laws of the land. That their only object was to dissolve the Union and destroy the best government on earth Declared that the whigs were abolitionists in disguise—a pack of hungry, howling and ravenous wolves dressed up in sheep's clothing bleating and begging for office. That they were worse, more detestible and meaner than the abolitionists, for they had neither the manhood nor the courage to avow their principles and convictions. That protection for American labor about which they had so much to say, was nothing but a scheme for robbing the poor man for the benefit of the rich. He then compared the merits of the presideutial candidates. Said that Gen. Scott had been properly named 'Old Fuss and Feathers' because he amounted to nothing. That Franklin Pierce of New Hampshire was a patriot, soldier and statesman of the very highest order. That if he were elected president of the United States he would enforce the fugitive slave law and protect the southern people in their inalienable constitutional and God-given rights to their property and thus preserve the Union as our fathers made it, from dissolution and destruction.

Having elaborated in his usual way each of the heads, which formed the substance of all Democratic speeches, in those days, he drew forth from his pocket a paper and said: "I am here charged in this paper which I hold in my hand, with having promised to secure Federal appointments for 23 worthy, reputable and in every way competent men, who live in this district. The editor not only makes the charges but has collected a great amount of evidence to prove it and for all that I can see, does prove it. Now I want to say right here, fellow-citizens, that if I have made these promises and this editor says, that I have and seems to have proven it, every one of these men shall be appointed. Every promise that I have made shall be fulfilled, if I am elected and I am sure I will be. And I say more, that there are a great many other competent and worthy men, who shall likewise receive appointments for I am determined, when I am elected that this district shall have its full share of the Federal patronage, some thing it never had yet. What is there wrong about that? Who will say this district should not have that which rightfully belongs to it. Even the editor of this paper, himself, will not dare say there is any wrong in that. And while I will always give the preferences to members of the Democrat party, as a matter of course, yet there are many worthy and competent men in the opposition who would fill positions with credit to themselves and their country."

The speech had the desired effect Applications, almost without number, from men of both parties were made and in all cases the promise was given to these patriots, that if, they would wor kand vote for him, that they should receive the desired appointment. Democrats and Whigs now, animated by the same hope and actuated by ths same motive vied with each other in their devotion to the Chieftian and his cause. His election way easy—but the appointments—

CHAPTER II.

His advent into Congress. His opposition to the Kansas-Nebraska bill. The understanding. He defies Senator Douglas The Senator pulls the wool over his eyes. The Chieftain and Senator both happy. He agrees to support the bill. Comes to Kansas. Organizes the Democratic party. His betrayal,and political downfall in the Democratic party. Joins the free-state men.

Soon after his advent into Congress he was confronted with the grandest and most adroit political swindles ever conceived by the mind of men,the bill for the organization of the territory of Kansas and Nebraska and the repeal of the Missouri compromise. That the south might force slavery into Kansas by fraud and murder and at the point of the bayonet if necessary. But such was the opposition to this bill throughout the country and especially in his own congressional district that for him to vote for it would be political suicide. This was rather more than he felt himself called upon to do, even in the interests of the Divine and constitutional institution of slavery. He,therefore,resolved to oppose it, notwithstanding it had been made an administration measure and a party test. The party lash was applied to him in vain. As the bill could not be carried without his support it became neccessary for Senator Douglas and the President to have an understanding with him.

THE UNDERSTANDING.

Senator.—Good evening, Colonel, I am really very happy to meet you tonight; but pardon me I should have said, general.

The Chieftain—Not at all, Senator, I can assure you that I am proud of my title of Colonel, and have no desire to be addressed by anything higher, until I am legitimately entitled to it.

Senator—All right then, Colonel, I can assure you that it is the general opinion of your countrymen that you honored the title while in Mexico. But, Colonel, I really owe you an apology for sending for you at this late hour in the night. I wished to see you on a matter of the utmost importance both to myself and the country and I wished the interview to be private. I understand that you are opposed to my bill for the organization of the territories of Kansas and Nebraska and the repeal of the Missouri compromise and I was anxious to see if I could not convince you that it would be to your interests to support my bill. You are aware, I suppose that it has been made an administration measure and consequently a test of fealty to the Democratic party.

The Chieftain—No apology at all. I can assure you, I deem it both a privilege and an honor to meet the Senator from Illinois at any time. I am aware that your bill has been made an administration measure and a party test. But, Senator, such is the opposition of my constituents to the repeal of the Missouri compromise that it would be nothing-short of political suicide for me to support your bill, and I cannot see what advantage it would be to belong to the Democratic party, if I am politically dead at home. True, I might receive an appointment and be a leach or sinacure on the government while this administration lasts; then be turned out, without honor or prospects, to be a dead duck the remainder of my life. Moreover, I am loyal to the platform of '52, on which the present administration was elected, and upon which it is in honor bound to stand. I, also, deny most emphatically the right to make any other test of Democracy.

Senator.—Very true, you are certainly, right, Colonel, there can be no other party test than fealty to that platform of sound Democratic principles. I myself had a great part in making that platform and will acknowledge no other test neither will any other true Democrat. My bill, also, is in perfect harmony with it. Are you not aware, Colonel, that the opposition, which you speak of, comes principally from the abolitionists, whig and disaffected Democrats and is but ephemeral and will soon pass away? At least, your senior Senator informs me such is the case.

The Chieftain—By no means. The opposition in my district comes from the Democrats, themselves. I can assure you I would care nothing for the opposition of the whigs and abolitionists. Nothing would give me more pleasure than to fight them. But I have letters from nearly all the leading Democrats of my district urging me to oppose the bill. Nearly all the papers of our party oppose the repeal of the Missouri compromise. The Democrats of all the largest towns in my district have held meetings and denounced the opening up of the slavery question (the writer was lecturing in his district at that time and knows this to be true). I have also written letters to many of my constituents telling them I would vote against the bill. I have no doubt in the world, Senator, but that I can be re-elected on the position I have taken.

Senator.—Colonel, when you are as old as I am you will be very careful how you write letters, pledging yourself to any course.

The Chieftain—Indeed, Senator, that was one of the very first political lessons taught me by my father and, if I am not as old as you are, I think I understand how, and when to write letters.

Senator.—I have the utmost confidence in the prudence and sagacity of your father and, if he has given you instructions on letter writing, you need no suggestions from me. (We all, here, recollect how he set the ball in motion for Jackson.) But you will pardon me, I think, Colonel, you are mistaken about your re-election, in opposition to my bill. You will be a bolting candidate and there will be a regular Democratic candidate and the opposition will have a candidate who may be elected.

HE DEFIES THE SENATOR AND THE ADMINISTRATION.

The Cheiftain—I have no desire. Senator, to pursue this subject further except to say that, under the circumstances, I cannot support your bill. Personally, I should be very glad to do so, but self preservation is the first law of nature and, however, much I may desire it, I cannot. That your bill has been made an administration measure and consequently a party test, I have been fully aware for some time, but you will pardon me, Senator, if I remind you, also, that unless your bill passes congress, the making it a party test will amount to nothing or be worse than folly; and, also, that it will take not only, my vote but that of several other Democratic members to carry it through, and that we have pledged ourselves to stand together. You must, also, pardon me, Senator if I tell you that politics sometimes makes strange bed-fellows. I comprehend the situation perfectly. To support your bill, Senator, would ruin me politically, forever. I am yet a young man, and have what I consider a laudable ambition to be somebody and so far, I have been as successful as I could expect, if not, as I could wish, as you yourself will allow and do not feel that it would be right or that I am called on to sacrifice myself and all my prospects, even for my best and most honored friend.

THE SENATOR PULLS THE WOOL OVER HIS EYES.

Senator—Certainly, certainly, Colonel you have been very successful so far, and for a young man of your ability there is no position in the country but what is possible for you. But to change the subject, Colonel, how would you like a seat in the senate?

The Chieftain—A seat in the senate should satisfy the ambition of almost any man, and to be frank with you, Senator, I am looking ahead at that at the proper time.

Senator—But, Colonel you certainly cannot expect to supplant Senator Bright and he is quite a young man yet. So the proper time as you term it, in your state, must necessarily be quite remote indeed.

The Chieftain—Very true, but there is no telling what may turn up, and my motto is be ready for anything that may turn up. Though as you say the prospect in my state seems remote, indeed.

Senator—We, Colonel that is the president and myself have a plan by which you can secure a seat in the senate, should it meet your views.

The Chieftain—What is the plan, Senator. Any means by which I can secure a seat in the United States senate, honorably, and you know Senator, what that means, will meet my views most certainly.

Senator—Ot course, honorably means successfully. We have it from reliable authority that the lands of Kansas are very fertile and attractive. Consequently there will be a great rush of people there to get possession of these lands both from the north and the South. The South will encourage emigration with the hope of making Kansas a slave state. The North with the expectation of making it a free state. Before the first summer passes away there will be people enough to form a state government and entitle Kansas to admission into the Union as a state. Now, we wish some first-class young man to go to Kansas and organize the Democratic party on the basis of the platform of '52 and superintend the organization of the state government and the admission of the state into the Union. For pioneer life, he must be a young man, and as most of the people will be from the western states he must be a western man. You are the best qualified and most suitable. Your opposition to my bill, is the only thing in your way. You shall have the support of the administration in the organization of the party, you will be the head of the party and have all the authority that two senators and a governor would have—More, you will be virtually dictator of the party there. All appointments and removals from office in the territory will be made upon your recommendation, and when the state government is formed you will be the administration candidate for the United States senate Then, with your prestige, you can dictate the other senator and come here clothed with all the power and authority of two senators, besides you can dictate the governor of the state and other state officers and that will give you a standing in the senate such as no other senator, except myself, will have.

The Chieftain—In what position shall I go there.

Senator—It would not be best for you to go there in any official capacity whatever. One holding official positions necessarily engenders enemies. Besides, Colonel, you could not be confirmed by the senate for any position You have expressed your opposition to the repeal of the Missouri Compromise and for that those Southern hounds will never forgive you, nor vote for your confirmation for any office whatever. The best way for you to go will be as a private citizen, take a claim as an honest yoeman,—you understand,—call for a mass convention of the Democracy of the territory as soon as possible and organize the Democracy on the platform of '52 The president will recognize your organization as the legitimate Democratic party of Kansas—You, of course, will have yourself made chairman of the Central committee. Further, you must apparently go on your own responsibility. If these Southern whelps find out, we, I mean the president and myself, have any responsibility in your going there, they will defeat my nomination for the presidency, though they have all pledged themselves to support me if I would introduce this bill and get Northern support enough to carry it through Congress. Under the opperation of my bill, which leaves the people of the territory perfectly free to settle the question of slavery in their own way, subject only to the constitution of the United States. Why the repeal of the Missouri compromise, only makes slavery possible in Kansas, but, not at all probable. These southern fellows, are fighting for a barren idiality, if they knew it. Nothing more. There is nothing practical about them. While one southern man would get there with his slaves, a dozen, Yes, I may say, a hundred men will go there from the North and West. Besides the right of holding slaves in the territories is left in obeyance for the courts, and, until that question is settled, no one will be so foolish as to take slaves into Kansas and run the risk of losing them. Therefore, under an impartial, fair and honest administration of my bill, in accordance with the constitution and principles as enunciated in the national Democratic platform of '52 Kansas will unquestionably become a free state. This will be to my interest—I foresaw all this opposition in the North, that you speak of in your district. But when Kansas comes into the Union as a free state, this opposition will all cease and I will have the unanimous support of the Northern Democracy. It will be necessary to have Kansas admitted, as a free state, before the next presidential election. Then everything will be just as I would have it. I will be president without a doubt, you will be a leading senator of the nation and should you desire anything else under my administration, you can have it. Or should you prefer the succession, after my second term, the influence of my administration will be at your disposel.. The president and I are in perfect accord in all these things and during his administration we will have his cordial support and co-operation. I have those southern rascals just where I want them. They thought they were playing it sharp. They supposed the repeal of the Missouri compromise would lay me out in the North, and then as a worn out tool that could be of no more service to them throw me aside. But they did not know with whom they were fooling. Colonel, all this is in the strictest confidence, I would not say these things to you, if I had not the most implicit confidence in your honor, not only, as a gentleman and a member of the Congress of the United States, but also, as a member of the Democratic party that which no tie can be more sacred and binding between honorable men—as we both profess to be. They will find their match this time, if they never did before. The repeal of the Missouri compromise, also, kills old Benton, my most influential and inveterate enemy.

He came into prominence on it and when it's repealed, don't you see, will end his career? You see I have looked the ground all over very carefully. It will be necessary for you, also, to mislead those southern scoundrels with regard to our plans on the slavery question and make them believe you are in favor of making Kansas a slave state. This you can do on your way to Kansas by stopping in Missouri and trying to buy some slaves to take with you to Kansas. As actions speak louder than words, this will have the desired effect. You need not conclude a bargain. You can ask time. Then it can be telegraphed over the country that you, on your way to Kansas, have stopped in Missouri to buy some field hands to take with you to that territory to open up your farm. Do you not see how carefully I have thought over the whole subject.

The Chieftain—I am, very much

impressed with what you say, Senator, but there is one difficulty in the way. I have been quite conspicuous in my opposition to your bill and should I now vote for it people would think and say I was bought and as I would have no official position they would very naturally conclude that money was the consideration and that would be most damaging to me, in my new field.

Senator—Just so, Colonel, but I have already thought of that, also, and have a way to obviate that objection. The President will instruct the Marshal of your state to get instructions from your constituents instructing you to vote for my bill on the ground that since they have seen my bill and understand it, that they are in favor of it, since it gives freedom to the territories as well as the states. He will also get letters from leading Democrats who have been opposing it, also clippings fromt he leading newspapers. You can thus vote for it under instructions. Personally, I take it, that you are like myself,—no sentiment in politics. Success is the only criterion by which we are governed and the only end to which we aim.

The Cheiftain—The argument, Senator, strikes me very favorably, I have no doubt but "John Lard Oil" can get the instructions, letters, and clippings you speak of, for he seldom fails in what he undertakes, but I would like to have the assurance of the president himself, that he will carry out all these things, just as you say he will. I do not doubt your word, in the least, but then I wish to have the assurance from him personally. I always make it a rule to be on the safe side both in business and politics.

Senator—John Lard Oil! What is the meaning of that Colonel? I don't understand it.

The Chieftain—Oh! it is simply a nickname we give the Marshal, John L. Robinson, because he has his whisky shipped to him in kegs, marked LARD OIL.

Senator—I see! About the assurance of the president. It would never do for you and I to go to the White House together to see him. Those southern whelps keep him literally besieged and should any of them see us go there for a private interview they would immediately surmise that something was up, and in some way defeat our object. But I thought you would want that assurance, so I have brought you a letter from the president, in the hand-writing of his private secretary in which, as you will see he pledges himself to carry out any arrangement I may make with you

The Chieftain—(reading the letter) That's all satisfactory.

Senator—Just you continue your

opposition and be more out spoken than ever, until the instructions arrive and then I will let you know when to come to the support of my bill. Everything is now understood and satisfactory is it.

THE CHIEFTAIN AND SENATOR BOTH HAPPY.

The Chieftain—Everything is satisfactory and I feel very grateful to you for the interest you have taken in my welfare, and when ever I can render you a service, call on me.

Senator—All right, Colonel, I will do so. I, also congratulate you, as the first senator from the future state of Kansas.

The Chieftain—I, also, congratulate you, as the next president of the United States, Good-night, Sena'o:.

Senator—Good-night, Colonel.

The Senator the next day, in the name of the president, wrote to the Marshal, who was ever equal to all emergencies of that kind, and in due time the desired instructions, letters and clippings arrived, as requested.

HE YIELDS HIS OPPOSITION.

Shortly before the passage of the bill when it became necessary to have his vote on the preliminary motions. The Chieftain made known the instructions and letters which he had received with all the apparent candor of one who believed them genuine. Stated that his chief reason for opposing the repeal of the Missouri compromise, was because he believed his constituents were opposed to it, but since he had learned that a great change, had recently taken place in their views, and that they were now strongly in favor of it, he would yield whatever private reasons he may have had and vote as his constituents had instructed and wished him to do. This he believed to be the true duty of a representative of the people.

HE GOES TO KANSAS.

The bill passed. The Chieftain gathering his effects and *Penates* little ones and bidding adieu to his friends and native land, loosed his "political" barque from its mooring in the scenes of his heretofore greatness and set sail on that vast and treacherous political sea, for Kansas and the Senate of the United States and ultimately the White House, the *ultima Thrul* of his ambition and bearing *imo pectore* great secrets of state' known only to two men besides himself, the president and the most distinguished senator in the nation; confiding also in their assurances that they would watch over and protect his litile barque until its fame should fill the whole land. A smile would then play over his countenance as he thought how nicely he was escaping the scalping knife of those disappointed patriots in his old district, who were crying for vengence and also congratulated himself that fortune had favored him and that he was going far beyond the reach of his enemies;nay more that he was a secret Envoy Extraordinary and Minister Plenenportetiary, a chosen and trusted Ambassador from among all chief men of the nation sent on the grandest and most important mission that could be entrusted to man; that of organizing the great Democratic party on the basis of those sound and truly Democratic principles, as enumerated in the national Platform of 1852 and laying the foundations of a great state and placing it where it would shine as a star forever on the banner of the Union, and also himself as the first senator holding council with the great and wise men of the nation. Finally he pictured himself seated in the president's chair and occupying fames topmost pinicle, receiving the plaudits of millions, both now "and yet to be."

He also applied the words of the poet with a slight change to himself

"While rivers into seas shall run,   [sun;
  The space of heaven round. the radiant
While trees, to mountain-tops with shades.
                      supply
  My honor name and fame shall never die"

HE STOPS IN MISSOURI

and makes known that he was on his way to Kansas, where he was going to live the life of a farmer and desired to open up his farm, but as he wished to purchase on time, he did not succeed his references probably not being satisfactory.

HE REACHES KANSAS.

and proceeds to Lawrence and locates a claim near the city and begins the life of an honest farmer among the "squatter sovereigns" of Kansas but soon after.

ORGANIZES THE DEMOCRATIC PARTY.

without any unnecessary delay he issued a call, for all those who believed in the doctrine and principles of the De-

mocratic party as enumerated in the
platform of 1852 to assemble in mass
convention in the city of Lawrence on
a given day for the purpose of organizing the Democratic party of the territory of Kansas. The place appointed for the meeting was a little log
house near the bank of the Kaw river.
The house was small compared with
the Herculian labor that was about
to be performed in it. But the inside
and outside would hold all that
would be likely to assemble and the
more there would be on the outside, the
greater would be the *eclat* of the convention. The time for the assembling
of the mass convention at length came
but the Democracy anxious for an
organization on the platform of '52
did not materalize to any great etxent
Six men including the Chieftain, himself, entered the building the Hon. S.
N. Wood who, in the opinion of many
people, came to Kansas at the instance

of Senator Chase of Ohio for a similar purpose on a very different platform from the one under consideration, he remained on the out side to watch the agony through a crack while, "*Ridiculus mus necitar.*" The Chieftain, nothing at all discouraged by the smallness of the number present with great dignity called the meeting to order, and stating the object for which the convention had been called, nominated one of the number for chairman of the meeting and put the vote and declared him unanamously elected. A secretary was then chosen. He now instructed the chairman to declare the meeting ready for business which was accordingly done. He then made a speech in his grandiloquent style on the importance of the great work that had called them together, and denounced the free-state men, as the offscouring and scum of Northern society who had been sent there by the Abolition Emigrant Aid societies for the purpose of controling the elections and making an abolition state of Kansas.

Next he moved that a committee of six be appointed on pre-amble and resolutions and instructed the chairman how to put the motion and the secretary how to make the record of it, and then instructed the chairman to appoint the committee, stating that "himself" as mover of the resolution according to parliamentary rule, should be appointed chairman of the committee. As chairman of the committee he got the six into the corner of the room and pulled forth from his pocket the whereases already prepared to the dotting of the i's and the crossing of the t's, and read them with great *gusto* to the committee. A motion was now made to adopt the pre-amble and resolutions as read and report them to the mass convention and recommend their adoption by that body. On motion the committee adjourned. The Chieftain now requested his chairman to take his seat and called the convention to order and taking a position in the midst of the floor said, Mr. Chairman your committee on pre-amble and resolutions would after due consideration beg leave to submit the following report and recommend its adoption by this mass convention of the people of Kansas, reads the pre-amble and resolutions, and then asked some one at his right to make a motion that the report be accepted and the committee discharged. This done, a motion was made that the report be now adopted by the convention. Another spread eagle speech, at the conclusion of which he told them it would be the proper thing for them all to wave their hats and shout at the top of their voices and make all the noise that they were capable of doing as soon as the chairman should announce the resolutions carried, all of which was carried out as suggested. When quiet was restored a Central committee of six was appointed of which the Chieftain, of course was chairman. The convention then adjourned *sini die*. He now took the records from the secretary, saying it would be necessary for him to have them, as he wished to make out a report of the proceedings for the press and rolling them up and placing them in his pocket departed for his abode thus the Democratic party of the territory of Kansas was organized and if ever a politician could be truly said to carry a whole party in his pocket, it was the Chieftain, as he walked away from that meeting

HE SOLIQUISES.

The convention was not large but his father held a convention with just half the number that proved successful and made Jackson. Why not this one be fully as successful. His published report of it would set everything forth in good shape, while the report that S. N. Wood would make, would be considered as and abolition lie. Besides he was the chosen representative of President Pierce and Senator Douglas to carry cut their plans and purposes. Nothing now was wanting but

THE RECOGNITION OF HIS

Democratic party by the administration at Washington which in good time was sure to come. It mattered not to him that Candle-box Calhoun and other pro-slavery officials denounced him as a traitor to true Democracy and an abolitionist. He could afford to exercise a dignified forbearance until the recognition should come, when the official heads of all those who did not bow to him and recognize his Democratic party, should fall into his political waste basket, and good and true men be appointed in their places. That the promises made to him by the president of the United States and Senator Douglas would turn like his promises to those who were now crying for political vengence in his old district and that with the same measure that he did mete it should be measured to him again, heaped up and running over at the sides, never once entered his mind.

THE RECOGNITION COMES,

but not the recognition of him and his party on the platform of '52. Rightly divining that Senator Douglas had sent him to Kansas to organize the Democratic party on the basis of the platform of '52, and thus bring Kansas into the Union as a free state, in order to promote his political prospects in the North, slavery compelled the president to recognize Candle-box Calhoun's dynasty, as the true Democracy of Kansas. And although, it was a matter of the most perfect indifference to the Chieftain, himself whether "slavery was legislated into Kansas or excluded therefrom or whether the people were left perfectly free to regulate their institutions in their own ways, subject only to the constitution of the United States, yet he had become a party to a policy that, if carried out, would make Kansas a free state. That was the unpardonable sin, for which there could be no forgiveness, though sought in penitence and tears. It seemed now as though bedlum had opened wide its mouth and was belching forth all its curses upon his head. He was denounced as the very arch-fiend of abolitionism. A price was set upon his head. Slavery was ever practical in its methods of dealing with opposition. If he had been some huge monster of a wild beast roaming over the prairies devouring all with whom he came in contact, he could not have been more feared and detested. Nor was the abuses confined to the slave state Democracy of Kansas alone. The Democracy of the whole country, congress, the president and Senator Douglass all united in declaring him an abolitionist, villain, murderer, scoundrel and full of all uncleanness and as a traitor to the true Democratic party which was the greatest of all crimes.

The condition of Gilderoy's famous kite was nothing to be compared to that of the Chieftain and his "Democratic party of '52." Both he and it were wrecked on the perilous billows and brakers of slavery,—he escaping with his life only. He was now in a similar condition to that of Elijah, when he was fed by the ravens only there were no ravens to feed him; or that of David, when Saul sought his life, without any Jonathan to befriend him; or, as those men of old, of whom it was declared that this world is not worthy, he wandered about not in a sheep skin or a goats skin as they did but in an old seal-skin coat, without their faith to support him.

"Whom of gods and men did he not accuse."

HE IS NOW DECLARED AN OUTLAW.

not only to the party of his choice but the party to which he had an undisputable birthright. All hope of honor and fame through that party is lost, lost forever.

"However grievious death may be," it was nothing to be compared to his present condition and suffering. Revenge he resolves upon, but how shall he obtain it? If he were only a Sampson, that he could lay hold of the pillars of the Democratic house, how gladly he would pull it down upon himself, if all in the house and especially those on the top should perish with him in the fall. That he could

not do. But, as the enemy of mankind "with his fallen peers" about him
'Lay vanquished. rolling in the firery, gulf
And nine times the space that measured day
                        and night
To mortal men."
plans the attack on Adam and Eve for the ruin of the human race and to avenge himselt for being
"Hurl'd headlong flaming from th' ethereal
                        sky,
With hideous ruin and combustion, down
To bottomless perdition, there to dwell;"
So, the Chieftain for many more
"Than nine times the space that measures
                    day and night"
Wanders about in his old sealskin coat, but alone, suffering as in.
"In adamantine chains and penal fire," and meditating revenge on the leaders and the party that had betrayed him until the thought strikes him. Slavery! Yes that's it! "To force slavery into Kansas,' I have been be-

trayed! Slavery! It is the very apple of their eye! The very ideal of their souls! The shrine at which they worship! Dearer to them than gold and silver and lands! Yes than wives and brothers and sisters fathers and mothers; than honor and fame and country! Dearer than all these! To destroy slavery will be to destroy the Democratic party and if it does not destroy the Democrats themselves it will render their condition more intolerable than, even death itself! Suffering all the horrors and agonies of death: longing and hoping for death; yet, cannot die! Dying always, yet, not dead! Also, a fearful looking for and expectation, beyond the grave, when death does come, of something more terrible, more dreadful, the sting and gnawing of the worm and the death that never dies! When they shall be dead to all hope, joy and happiness, but alive to dispair, misery and wretchedness only. Always dying but never dead! Always burning, but never consumed! Ever starving yet cannot eat, and forever thirsting but cannot drink! Oh how pleasing the thought! It is joy unspeakable, music to my very soul! It's all right now! I've got it at last! I will wage an eternal war upon slavery It, henceforth, shall be the object of my wrath. Upon it I will pour out the full measure of my vengence. Kansas is the rock upon which slavery shall be broken, and the recoil of the shock shall not only, drive it from the Union, but eventually, from the face of the earth, and in the conflict, which must ensue, I shall lead great armies and fame and glory shall be mine. No prouder memorial could be inscribed on the humble stone, that may mark my last resting place, or the monument that freemen shall erect than "The Avenger of the Down Troden of the earth.'

Now at any other time and under any other circumstances, the Chieftain who had been trained from his youth to look upon the abolitionists as the most execrable and despicable of all men, would as a matter of choice, just as soon, have thought of entering the sulphury regions and with Belzebub and his cohorts waging war upon Michael and the arch-angles, as to think of joining the free state men, to make war with them on slavery. He never had made a speech but what they came in for a full share of his vituperations, nor could he find words in the vocabularies of the human tongue sufficient to express his detestation and abhorance in which he held them and their principles. This in his estimation was the sum, substance and the very essence of a truly Democratic speech, and the only standard by which it could be prepared and without which there could be no excellence in it, whatever. And, though, he had never killed or stoned them, yet, like Saul, when the martyr Stephen was stoned, yet he was always ready to hold the clothes of those who did.

For him, therefore, to think of joining those, whom, he had been so recently declaring were abolitionists in disguise and calling them everything to which he could lay his tongue was worse tenfold than swallowing wormwood and gall. The question, also, arose in his mind would they admit him, and, if they should, there was one among them, who Goliah-like, stood head and shoulders above all other men in that party, and who was not only honored and respected for his prudence, courage and ability, but was almost idolized and adored by the people of the territory. Such was Dr. Charles Robinson, familiarly called Charley, at that time, the distinguished leader of the free-state men of Kansas. Him he could not hope or expect to supercede, but for the present, he could work under him, in some subordinate position until the proper time came for the election of United States Senators then, while Charles Robinson would undoubtedly be one of them, he could probably be the other. If so he could then meet on equal terms the great Senator from Illinois, and demand personal satisfaction in mortal combat on the field of honor, according to the code. His experience in Mexico, he thought, since there did not appear to be any one among the free-state men who had any military knowledge, would be of service to them in the approaching conflict and would also be an inducement for them to receive him.

There was, however, no alternative, and as, Esther resolved to go unbidden into the presence of the king, so he resolves unasked to unite with the free-state party. Perhaps they might bid him come, but if he perished he could only perish there,

"To stay away he must forever die."

In the city of Lawrence, there was but one man, in whom the Chieftain thought he could confide. To him he made known his purpose to unite with the free-state party at their next meeting, which was soon to be held; and requested, as a personal favor that he would call on him for a speech.

THE MEETING.

In rather a rude hall but as good as the City of Lawrence could afford in those early times, were assembled together quite a number of settlers, very similar in appearance to laboring men in their ordinary working clothes. These men must not, however, be judged by their appearance. At that early day nearly every sixth man, in this young and enterprising abolition city was the possessor of a diploma from some college or other institution of learning, that had the right to confer such honors, while the rest had nearly all secured a good common school or liberal education. To find any one who could not both read and write and converse fluently and intelligently on all subjects of current events and common interest was a rare occurence indeed. Some in that meeting were known throughout the country as discreat, couragous and able leaders and the body as awhole would compare most favorably with any state legislature in the country, if not with the Congress of the United States. Men in that meeting have since filled every position of honer and trust in the state. Men there that have represented the people in Congress. Some also have filled important places in the army and distinguished themselves as soldiers on hard and well fought battlefield, where many sealed, with their devotion to the holiest of all causes—that of truth and freedom.

Charles Robinson afterwards the first governor of Kansas was there;also Gen. G.W. Deitzler and Colonel Samuel Walker and others who, afterwards immortalized their names at Wilson Creek, where the ever to be lamented Lyon fell; Hon. S. C. Pomeroy, since United States Senator; Hons, Martin F. Conway and Sidney Clarke who have since represented the state in Congress; Dr. Day;Judge J. S. Emery who soon after visited many cities and laid the political situation of the free-state men before the people of the country and has since been United States Attorney. Shaler W. Eldridge the well known hotel man. and brothers. Asaph and Luther Allen who served as Captians during the war of the rebellion. Allen the Hardware man, since adjutant general of the state of Kansas. Simpson

Bro's the bankers, who confined their attention to their business and never sought political distinction; Hoyt the martyr;Banscomb who has since served in the Legislature of Kansas, also of Missouri; Messrs Hendry and Miller who have since been State Senators; Wm Hutchison; Hon. S. N. Wood, the irrepressible who has since been an important factor in the history of Kansas; Hon. Wm. E. Phillips correspondent of the New York Tribune, since Colonel in the army,member of Congress; The brave and fearless Jenkins, who was afterwards killed in a quarrel with General Lane; Mr. Whitney of the Whitney House. There were also many others present whose names cannot be recalled, but none the less worthy of mention on that account. Memory may also be at fault as to some of the names mentioned.

HE COMES TO THE MEETING.

The Grim Chieftain 63

Into this gathering of Free-state worthies, whose fame will endure while noble and heroic deeds shall find a lodging place in the memory of mankind, the Chieftain, clad in his old seal skin coat, came, and going to the back part of the hall, took his seat there, while, those present looked at him with astonishment, then at each other, wondering, no doubt, in their minds, whether Satan had come also.

HE IS CALLED ON FOR A SPEECH.

During the progress of the meeting after several speeches had been made Mr Miller, with who he had previously made the arrangement to call on him for a speech, arose and said, that he saw Col ———— and that he, for his part, should be very much pleased to hear something from him, if he should see fit to favor them with his views. Scarcely were the words out of his mouth, before the Chieftain, to prevent them from choking him off in any way if they should feel so disposed sprang to his feet and without waiting for recognition by the chairman, began speaking—stupefied and amazed the audience silently heard him through.

THE SPEECH.

No report can do justice to the vituperation and anathemas that he poured fourth onto the heads of these "Hell hounds" of slavery as he called the slave-state Democracy and Senator Douglass and the president, who, he declared, had resolved, by fraud, violence and murder, and by the whole power of the general government, even at the point of the bayonette if necessary to force slavery into Kansas contrary to the known will and wishes and against the most earnest and solemn protest of her people who had under the organic law of the territory had the sole right of determining what institutions should be and whether or not they wanted slavery.

"No horrid thing did his tongue refuse."

He concluded by declaring that from now henceforth and forever or as long as he lived, that he was one with them—a crusader for freedom. That the war was to the knife and the knife to the hilt and the death until slavery and everything that upheld it should be swept to distruction and wherever the battle would rage the fiercest and hottest, with them he would always be found, in any position, in which they might see fit to place him, though it were only a private in the ranks.

CHAPTER III.

His political rise and downfall in the free state party, Historical sketch. Kansas invaded by armed hordes from Missouri. First or bogus Legislature. Bogus code. Energy and zeal of the Chieftain in the free-state cause. He is chosen commander-in-chief of all the free-state rorces. Dr. Root's address informing him of his appointment. His reply. The horror of all horrors. His army. How he armed his men. His uniform as commander-in-chief. Captain Cook of the U. S. Army fails to recognize him in his uniform. The fear and terror of his name in Missouri. He visits Missour in disguise as Rev. Dr. Foote. Preaches to them and exhorts them to drive the abolitionists out of Kansas. Visits Lexington Mo., in the disguise of a stone mason. He visits the states,

That the reader may have a clear understanding of his career which was so intimately blended with the early history of Kansas it will be neccessary to give a brief sketch of that period

Under the direction of no less a personage than the acting vice president of the United States, Daniel R. Atchison, armed men from Missouri invaded Kansas and took forcible possession of all the voting precincts and elected the members of the first territorial legislature, many of whom were residents of Missouri. This action, they claimed was strictly in accordance with the organic law which provided that every person, passing certain qualifications and who should be in the territory on the day of the first election, should be a qualified voter at said election. "We," said they "are here, therefore, we are voters."

The law did not prescribe that each person should vote but once, therefore they could vote as often as they chose. They voted and took a drink and voted again, voted and treated and voted again; voted and walked around the house and voted again; voted and changed coats and voted again; voted and swapped jack knives and voted again; voted took off their coats and voted in their shirt sleeves, then put on their coats and voted again; voted changed hats and voted again; voted and forgot they had voted and voted again; and called on the abolitionists that it was a perfectly free election and that all whosoever would, could vote without money and without price and voted again; voted and shook hands, they were so happy, and voted again. What a glorious election that was! How the soul of every true Democrat was rejoiced and made glad on that day. In this way the practical workings of the great Democratic boon of "Squatter Sovereignty," that neither legislated slavery into the territories nor excluded it from them but left the people to regulate their own institutions in their own way subject only to the constitution of the United States were exemplified and made manifest at the first election in the territory of Kansas.

This great army provided with all the machinery and appliances for holding and carrying the election, such as judges, clerks, candidates, returning officers, poll-books, tally-sheets and what ever might be needed and strong and numerous enough to seize all the voting places was organized under their very eyes and must have had the assurance of the official and material support of the administration or it never would have been attempted. The sequel shows that it had both and that the true intent and meaning of the repeal of the Missouri Compromise was to leave the people of Missouri perfectly free to force slavery into Kansas in their own way subject only to the will of David Atchison and his chief conspirators.

When this "bogus" legislature was convened it enacted a slave code for Kansas in a manner that for simplicity was almost sublime, by enacting that the word Missouri wherever it occurred in the code of that state should be be construed and held to mean Kansas. Kansas had, now, as black a slave code as ever darkened the pages of the statute book of any age or country for the American institution of slavery was the most abominable system that ever disgraced the face of the earth. The bondage of the children of Isreal in the land of Egypt, compared with it for barbarity and cruality was mild indeed. When this "Bogus" legislature had appointed all the county and other offices even down to justices of the peace, the new dispensation of the

GOSPEL OF THE FREEDOM OF THE TERRITORIES

was fully ushered in and that it might be permanently and firmly established forever the people were commanded that all things whatsoever were written in the book of this law, that they must observe and do to the end that there might be peace and happiness in the land. But the people said: "This law is a strange law unto us, not our law and we will obey none of its precepts nor commandments; neither shall there ever any bondsmen nor bondswomen dwell among us." And when they saw the smoke of their dwellings and towns and cities rising up unto heaven and there was sore oppression in the land, because they had no respect unto the law, they said unto the Chieftain: "You were great in war, in a far away country, come, go to, now and lead us to battle against these our enemies that we may slay them if so be it and deliver the land from this sore oppression and peradventure, we slay them not, that we may drive them hence even unto their own country. And it came to pass, when the Chieftain had led them forth to battle that they prevailed against their enemies mightily and smote them, so that they were not able to stand before them and their hearts melted within them and they were filled with great fear and trembling so that they fled even unto their own country. So now unto this day there was no respect for that law in all the land; neither are there any bondsmen or bondswomen therein. Then all the people, said one to another: "Great is the Chieftain who has made so great a deliverence" and they said unto him: "Because thou hast done this thing and brought such destruction and disgrace upon our enemies and didst make their very hearts quake within them, so that they dare not so much as show their faces in our land, for very fear, thou shalt hence forth be called THE GRIM CHIEFTAIN, and thou shalt continue to go in and out before us and we will honor and obey all thy commandments and precepts until we get a law of our own and even then thou shalt still continue to be great among us."

Whenever an invasion would occur he was naturally chosen to lead, as he was the only military man of any prominence among the free-state men. At length he is chosen

COMMANDER-IN-CHIEF

of all the free-state forces of Kansas, and Rev. A. P Root was made chairman of the committee, to wait on him and inform him of his appointment.

Dr. Root: "General, it affords me, as well as the committee of which I have the honor to be chairman great pleasure to inform you that the people of Kansas, reposing especial confidence in your prudence, skill and ability, as a military leader, have, by the only authority which they recognize, appointed you, commander-in chief of all the free state forces of to make arrests. The free-state legislature of Kansas was dispersed at the point of the bayonette and Gov. Robinson cast into prison on some fabulous pretext. The Chieftain's friends in his old congressional district, who never got their appointments, took this opportunity 'to get in their work' and joined in the fray. His life moral social, domestic, political and religious was overhauled from his cradle and depicted in the blackest colors and spread before the country as the unbiased testimony of those who knew him best.

HIS ARMY

consisted of men on their farms or claims and in the workshops, slaves and officers

"Who would leave their plowshares in the mould,
Their flocks and herds without a fold,
Their corn have garnered on the plain,"

and rally to their Chieftain's call in such numbers that the Missourian seemed to think that he possessed the fabled power of Pompey, the great, and could, by stamping his foot on the ground, raise up armies out of the earth.

HOW HE ARMED HIS MEN.

On one occasion, he made a call for men to drive out a company of Missourians, who were building a block house and molesting and running off the free-state settlers from that neighborhood. Many men came without arms expecting that he could in some way, furnish them. Apparently, taking no notice of the fact, he gave the command to fall in and follow him. When they had marched some distance, Capt. Aseph Allen and some one else, supposing that it was an oversight that the men were not provided with arms, sought the Chieftain at the head of the column and asked: "What are the men going to do for arms?" Suddenly stopping and crime which completely unfitted him for membership in the Democratic party; to join the abolitionists or free state party was as far as human depravity could go; but to appear in a full coat of war paint as chief of the abolition army, with his bow ready strung in his hand, his quiver well filled with barbed and poisoned arrows flung over his shoulder, tomahawk and scalping knife at his side, driving the minions of slavery before him as chaff is driven before the wind was the unspeakable horror of all horrors, the most horrible; the horror that should be despised by all true Democrats, from the very bottom of their souls. To them he was the very abomination of slavery or some worse if possible set up in the most holy place of slavery. Frantic and urgent appeals were made throughout the slave-holding states for men and money to aid in driving from Kansas or exterminating the inhuman and unearthly monster and his abhored horde of followers or slavery would be forever lost and the country ruined. Increased rewards were offered for his head, one in Alabama of $100,000. The Northern Democrats took up the howl and were not behind their Southern brethern in nothing save raising men and money, yet strange as it may seem now a company of men was raised in Pennsylvania and sent to help make Kansas a slave state but deserted when they learned the nature of the work they were required to do. Congress the president and cabinet came to the rescue of slavery, proclamations and manifestoes were issued; charges of treason were prefered against the Chieftain and leaders of the free-state men. Law and order parties invading Kansas from Missouri were the order of the day; army officers and United States Marshals were ordered

Kansas, and have delegated this committee to inform you of the fact."

The Chieftain straightening himself to his full height and with all the gravity and dignity of one who might be supposed to wear the diadem of the universe, replied: "Mr. Chairman, and gentlemen of the committee, allow me to say to you and through you, to the people of Kansas, that this is the proudest, as well as, the happiest moment of my life. Were the honors of the entire world at your disposal, you could not confer on me, one that would be more consonant to my feelings and wishes. It fills the measure of my ambition and my most cherished hopes and aspirations. To be commander-in-chief of the free men of Kansas and with them drive the murderous invading hords of the Democracy and slavery from her soil back to Missouri where they belong is a position of which any man should feel proud, since it is the highest and the noblest honor and the grandest glory that can fall to the lot of mortal man.

Allow me, Mr. Chairman, to say further, that words utterly fail to express the thanks and gratitude with which I accept the trust and honor that has been confered on me. All the energy, skill and ability which I possess shall be devoted to the cause which lies so near to the heart of all the people until the last armed invader who would inflict that blithing and withering scourge and curse of human slavery, is forever driven from the face of our beautiful territory."

Horor horrorum horrendissimus

To attempt to carry out a policy that would surely make Kansas a free state under an honest administration of the organic law of the territory and the national Democratic platform of 1852, the last expression of the policy and principles of that party was a looking them sternly in the face as though he was perfectly surprised at their stupidity, replied: "Why take them from the enemy." and marched on. When he came near to the camp of the enemy, he sent a free-state man ahead, and instructed him to run into their camp and tell them he was coming with his whole army and also to offer his service to them and tell them that he had served during the Mexican war, as a gunner and request to be put in charge of a cannon which the Chieftain knew they had. The free-state men did as instructed and took charge of the cannon without waiting to be formally installed as gunner saying he was go to blow the abolitionists to pieces.

While they were coming up the road, and began giving orders to the men what they should do. Just then the free-state men came in sight " on the double quick." Everything in that camp was confusion worse than confounded. The cannon by some means went of prematurely, tearing the top off the block house, while the Missourians started "pell mell, helter skelter" for their lives, leaving most of their arms and all their camp equipments and baggage. When the arms were distributed to the free-state men, the Chieftain walked up to Capt. Allen, as cool and unconcerned, as though nothing unexpected had occurred, and said; "Now, you see how it is done."

HIS UNIFOR AS COMMANDER-IN-CHIEF.

While he was ever ready and eager to resist to death the bogus militia, and sheriffs and all processes for his arrest by virtue and authority of the "bogus code, yet for the purpose of avoiding arrests by United States army officers and deputy marshals with whom it was his fixed policy never to come into conflict believing, as he always said, the moment that there was a collision with the United States authorities, everything was lost, he procured a uniform, that, for variety of colors and material would compare favorably with Joseph's famous coat of many colors though not so bright or gay. This consisted of a red wig with hair extending down his back over his shoulders and beard of the same color, covering his breast, both beard and wig looking as though they had never been either cleaned or combed, of an old crownless and rimless hat, above which the red hair of the wig extended; an old coat and pants and vest, covered over with old patches of every variety of material and color, sewed on with every variety of thread and for buttons, strips of old cloth, were run through the button holes of one side of the garments and holes punched in the other side and tied in an awkward knot; one old boot, on, one foot and an old shoe on the other with a club in his hand or on his shoulder. His appearance was somewhat similiar to what one might imagine that of the mythical ferryman that carries the departed shades over the river styx

"To night's Plutonian shore."

Dressed in this uniform, the value of which was equal to his salery, for a full year, as commander-in-chief, and under an assumed name, he would march in the ranks without being recognized by those most intimate with him. Judge Wakefield's sons, told the writer, that they marched with him for two days, one along side of him part of the time, and did not know at the time, he was in the command, though, they knew him perfectly well when not disguised. Though he carried a club, yet under that old coat was concealed a perfect arsenal of death, a full half dozen of the best revolvers that could be procured.

CAPTAIN COOK OF THE U.S. ARMY FAILS TO RECOGNIZE HIM.

He moved on Lecompton once on some business of importance but was prevented from carrying his designs into execution by Capt Cook whom he met there with his company. Capt. Cook who had orders for his arrest drew up his company in front of the Chieftain's forces and then rode all around them scrutinizing every man very closely and coming to Marcus J. Parrot inquired for the commander of those forces. "I have that honor" replied Mr Parrot. "It is my duty" replied the Captain "to command those men to disperse and return to their homes." "You shall be obeyed with pleasure" replied Mr Parrot and all started for their homes.

Capt Cook knew the Chieftain well having served with him in Mexico but failed to recognize him in his uniform though within a few feet of him while

talking to Mr. Parrot.
THE TERROR OF HIS NAME IN MISSOURI.
was realy frightful and inconceivable. The writer had some business about that time over in Missouri and staid all night with a farmer, though not a slave holder, not far north of Plattsburg. After supper he began conversation by asking the writer where he came from and where he was going. Very pointed questions under the circumstances the writer thought, but after answering in a manner that he flattered himself the great Talleyrand would have envied, could he have heard it. The Missourian seemed satisfied and continued the conversation in a very frank and friendly manner Soon he remarked: "They are having great trouble over in Kansas." This news appeared to be very astonishing and the writer inquired where Kansas was, if it was in Missouri. "No" said

he, looking as though he pitied the writers knowledge of geography "Kansas is the territory west of Missouri. Congress gave it to the south for a slave state but the abolitionists have gone there in great numbers to make it an abolition or free-state. And as it could not be made a slave state, while they were there, our people went over to drive them out. I never went over but I was afraid they would make me go. The abolitionists fought our men and drove them back. They have a general who was a Colonel in the Mexican war for a leader or commander. He is over eight feet high and well built in proportion and when he was commanding in Mexico, his voice could be heard all over the battle field above the roaring of the cannon. Stranger this is the God's truth I'm telling you. He has his men armed with Yankee guns, called Sharps rifles, that will shoot sixty times a minute and kill a man a mile away.

The Grim Chieftain 87

Our people thought they could drive them out with cannons, but they have now got cannons over there. some Yankee invention I suppose that they load by putting the balls in a hopper, the same as a miller puts grain into a hopper, to grind.—I can't discribe it to you or tell you how it works. I do not think the abolitionists can be got out and the south must loose Kansas."

Another night the writer was told that when the Chieftain took any of the Missiourians as prisoners he made them dig their own graves and then had them shot and buried them in the graves which they then selves had dug

HE VISITS IN MISSOURI AS THE REV. MR. FOOT OF ALABAMA.

When there were no bands of Missourians that required his attention,to avoid arrest by army officers and U. S. Marshals and wishing to become acquainted with the country thinking it might become necessary, at some time to follow the invaders across the line and carry the war into their own country he would visit Missouri in disguise. On one occasion under the assumed name of the Rev. Mr. Foot of Alabama, he traveled for quite a while in that state telling them of their duty in the present crisis to make Kansas a slave state, by driving out or exterminating the abolitionists. That is if they did not do so their slaves would be sent free and they and their wives and sons and daughters would be compelled to work like "niggers." And not only that but niggers" would marry their sons and daughters. That it was absolutely necessarry to make Kansas a slave state in order to secure the institution of slavery. That it was their duty to themselves and their families as well as their duty to their God, at all hazzards and by every means within their reach to drive out or kill that great arch-fiend of abolitionism (himself.)

He claimed to the writer that the sermon he preached one Sunday was considered by his congregation orthodox on the slavery question and that he was highly complimented for it. Those who knew the Chieftain will think he would be rather out of place in the pulpit delivering a sermon. But when it was recollected that nearly all Democratic speeches of those times were made principally of extracts from the sermons of southern preachers on the blessings and divinity of slavery and that the Chieftain had been a very prominent Democratic orator, it will be readly seen that he could make some very salient points if not a logically connected discourse

HE VISITS LEXINGTON MO. DISGUISED AS A STONE MASON HUNTING WORK.

At another time he landed from the deck of a steamboat at the city of Lexington, disguised with the grey, almost white wig and beard, the hair being quite long, carrying a kit of stone mason's tools and walked all over and around the city hunting work but no doubt, like the nigger, praying earnestly that he would find none. Had the people of Lexington known he was there it is hard to tell whether they would have run away in a panic or tried to take his life. Probably they would have thought he had a great army concealed and run.

HE VISITS THE STATES.

When the Missourians stopped

emigration and supplies from the north to Kansas at Lexington Mo. by stopping the steamboats to that city and sending back free-state emigrants and confiscating such property as they considered contraband with his usual sagacity he foresaw that unless there was some other route, by which emigration and supplies could come to Kansas, that the free-state was hopelessly ruined. He, therefore, visited a number of Western states and cities and laid before the people the true condition of affairs in Kansas directed that emigration should be through the state of Iowa, returning himself in that way with about three hundred settlers, most of them, men with their families teams and household effects; while a few thought there would be no baggage needed in Kansas but Sharps rifles and good navy revolvers. This company of emigrants was magnified by the proslavery Democracy of Missouri and the country into an immense army marching through Iowa. Some paper put it as high as 20.000 and some 50.000. He did all he could to keep up the impression. For when he could not be fighting or chasing the slave Democracy his next greatest glory was to be scaring them to death.

CHAPTER IV.

He runs David R. Atchison the acting Vice President of the United States with his free-booters and cut throats back to Missouri.

All attempts to crush out the free state men by armed bodies from Missouri having failed David R. Atchison, president of the Senate and acting vice president of the United States and the invisible head and grand moving spirit of the slave holding conspirators, resolved to raise and place himself at the head of an army commensurate with his own self supposed importance and dignity, that would speedly crush out all opposition to making Kansas a slave state. Having accordingly, collected from all parts of Western Missouri a number of men, variously estimated at, from twelve hundred, to three thousand and having thoroughly organized and equiped them he marched them into Kansas with the avowed purpose of exterminating or driving the abolitionists, as he called the free-state people, from the territory. For some reason or other, he camped soon after he crossed the line, probably to await the arrival of more men and supplies, but more probably to observe and see what effect his exalted personage and confidently supposed invincible force would have on the people. For it is only reasonable to suppose that some spark of humanity yet remained in his bosom and that he would rather scare them to death than kill them outright. Since Atchison was acting under no legal authority, the status of both him and his men in the eyes of the civilized world and by the laws of nations, was that of enemies of the human race freebooters and pirates, subject to be captured and put to death by any people or nation that had the power and saw fit to do so. It was the duty of Missouri to prevent these men from leaving the state and in case she neglected or was unable to do so it was the duty of the general government to protect the people of Kansas from their ravages but on the contrary these men had the active assistance and coöperation of the state authorities of Missouri in their behalf and the sympathy and moral and material support of the government of the United States. Many of them were armed with guns that were taken from the United States arsenals for the purpose.

To meet and repel this invasion the Chieftain hastily collected three hundred and fifty men, mostly from Lawrence and Douglas county, and set out for the camp of Atchison with all possible haste. He was compelled to act thus promptly to elude the United States troops whose officers had orders to arrest him and disperse his men, but strange to say, never had any orders to disperse the Missourians and arrest their leaders. They could roam over the territory at their will and commit depredations and burn and murder to their hearts content and their was no one, so far as the general government was concerned to molest or make them afraid. Had he delayed to collect larger force, he feared the troops would be thrown between him and enemy, as had been done on several occasion before, and thus cover and protect Atchison and be ready to arrest him and disperse his men. For these and other sound military reasons which will be apparent on reflection, it was indispensible that he should strike at once such a blow as would send Atchison back and let his men return to their homes. He, therefore, left Lawrence early in the morning and marched forty-four miles in one day and part of the night—three days march for an army in one— and halted for the remainder of the night about four miles from Atchisons camp.

What is the issue to be settled by these two armies when they meet in the morning?

If Atchison prevails the people of Kansas will be butchered or driven houseless, homeless and penniless from the territory and Kansas will be made a slave state and a slave-holding Oligarchy established on the ruins of the Republic. On the other hand if the free-state men drive back the invaders, any other attempt of the kind will be impossible, the people of Kansas will be secure in their homes and Kansas made a free-state, and the design to establish an Oligarchy over this continent with slavery as the cheif corner stone will be thwarted and slavery, itself, will be destroyed. No greater issue for good or evil was ever submitted to the grandest and mightiest armies that have ever shook the earth with their "trod.

Reader, if you were not one of that little army let your imagination carry you back to the place where those men stopped for the night to eat their scanty rations, and wait for the coming morning before they began their work of death. See the Cheiftain with his body inclined forwards and his head downward walking backward and forwards among his men, as they sit round in little groups talking of their coming fate, as though he was perfectly unconscious of everything. Imagine you hear him soliloquizing; "The coming morning brings the crisis of Kansas and my life Yes, it will settle the fate of Kansas and seal my destiny for weal or for woe. If I fail the people of Kansas will be butchered and driven out. Kansas will be a slave state, and a slave-holding Oligarchy take the place of the Republic. To fail, now this morning will be to fail forever, for I have no subsistency for my men, the troops will be here. The blow must be struck with the coming light. If I drive him,—all will be well; no other invasion can be made. They will be so utterly demoralized that they never can recover. Kansas will be a freestate, and the attempt to establish a slave-holding Oligarchy will be abandoned.. For Kansas is the natural key to that position. They will then attempt to dissolve the Union and set up a slave-holding government of the Southern States. This will make war and slavery will be destroyed and the Democratic party and its leaders will go down with it and the desire of my soul for revenge shall than be satisfied. The time is at hand and cannot be defered. I will this day rise to the very pinnacle of honor and fame, or die a most glorious death, which is far preferable to a life without hope and without prospects. Such a life I care not

to live—I cannot—I will not live.
If Atchison drives me back—no
that cannot —must not be. I will
drive him or I and all my men
will die a death that will render us
immortal, though dead we shall
live forever. Thermopylæ and
Kansas! Leondas and myself! If
I only had my revenge on Senator
Douglas and the Democratic party,
I think I should prefer such a
death with the assurance of immortal
glory to the uncertainties of
life. The opportunity is before
me and I will improve it. But
daylight will soon be here I must
talk to the men and get them ready.

By the very first appearance of
daybreak he had his men in motion,
soon came in sight of Atchison's
scouts or pickets. It is said
that Dol Donophan a man of considerable
experience, having, made
during the Mexican war, an expe-

dition almost equal to that of Cyrus the Younger and had been victorious in various battles, was in command of this scouting party. No fitter man could have been selected for the position. The selection by Atchison, of the man who carried the military brains of the expedition, for this post shows the great dread in which he stood of the Chieftain and his army and the great importance he placed upon reliable information as to his numbers, equipments and contemplated movements. It would be very natual to suppose that a man of his ability and experience could reconnoiter, almost at a glance, the number and capabilities of any force that was likely to be brought against him; but from strange and unaccountable reasons he magnified this little force of three hundred and fifty men into an army that were to be numbered not by thousands but by tens of thouands. Whether this ludicious and fatal mistake resulted from the scouts being in a condition to *see double* or from a terror-stricken imagination or from a sort of a mirage that sometimes apparently multiplies objects in the distance especially in the early twilight of the morning or whether it was caused, as some say, by the Chieftain, who, seeing the scouts as he was crossing a ridge or knoll, countermarched the head of his column, as soon as it decended out of their sight, through a low place, the ground favored the manœvre and strategy, brought it to the rear and then kept marching round and round in a circle continually moving over the high place towards the enemy and returning through the low places, thus seemingly magnified his numbers in the sight of the scouts for the purpose of producing a panic and demoralization in the camp of Atchison when they reported—Whether it was any one or all of these causes combined or some providential interference, that caused the mistake cannot be told.

As soon as the scouts left their position, the Cheiftain moved forward with all possible speed for the purpose of attacking Atchison while forming into position, at long range with his Sharp's rifles and when panic persued to rush on them with their revolvers, and put them to flight. Most of the free-state men carried from one to three pair of the best that could be procured. When, however, the free-state men came onto a rise of ground where they expected to see the enemy they saw only a cloud of dust moving towards Missouri. They had fled. The scouts ran in just as Atchison had taken off his hat to eat his breakfast and reported: "They are coming, not only by thousands, but by tens of thousands." Atchison seizing his hat and putting it on his head said; "We must either fight or run, I tell you that horrid monster coming will fight." And without telling his men which they must do, mounted his horse and made for Missouri on his best possible time, and his example was followed by all his men.

The freestate men found a breakfast already cooked in his camp and other property sufficient to make their little campaign a financial success. They pursued, till they made sure Atchison had gone to Missouri, and then returned to their homes.

What the result of a battle would have been had Atchison not fled, it may be useless to speculate. But, when we consider that, in addition to his bravery and mania for battle, and his desire for revenge on the leaders of his old party, the 'chieftain was playing for what he considered the grandest prizes that could fall to the lot of man, a Senatorship and the Presidency of the United States with all the honors and emoluments which these positions imply, it will not be unreasonable to conclude that Atchison would have been driven back or he and his army would have lost their lives in the attempt. This was the opportunity of his life and he knew it. To be defeated or fall back under any circumstances, no matter what the odds were against him would have been the ruin of all his most cherished dreams, hopes and aspirations. To him, than this, death would have been far preferable. There can be no doubt but that he was ready and willing then and there, as he always had been, to offer up his life, as a sacrifice on the alter of his ambition. That his men would have stood by him and shared his fate none but a simpleton can doubt. They had met and defeated and put to flight this same enemy, only in numbers not so great, on many other battle fields, as at Franklin, Black Jack, Ossowatomie, Hickory Point and other places. And many of those men since at Wilson Creek under Generals Deitzler and Bob Mitchell, and on many other hard fought battlefields, have, by their conduct added lustre to our national history. These men, after they had turned the business ends of there Sharp's

Rifles onto the enemy and thrown him into confussion, would have rushed into close quarters and vied with the chieftain, himself, in deeds of valor and daring until the coinage would have ended by the flight of the invaders or the death of the free-state men. They were out on a business trip that morning and ment no foolishness whatever.

The temptation to burlesque the ridiculous ending of this campaign on the part of Atchison, by throwing it into the machine, though a poor one and long out of use and much out of repair, and grinding it into verses, is too strong to be resisted:

   The Senator sat near his tent,
While musing on the expected hour,
The Chieftain in supplication bent,
Should tremble and implore his power

   But from these very pleasing though's:
This most delightful severy seeming,
He soon was roused, by frantic shouts
Of tenor stricken pickets screaming.

The Grim Chieftain 109

Before the morning dawn appeared
As, summer leaves in numbers seem,
That wiley Chieftain's army feared
Beyond that farther hill we've seen.

And as ravening wolves pursuing prey,
With each, the other vieing, run;
So eager for the expected prey,
His army in countless thousands come.

And soon, we, scattered o'er this plain,
Shall lie: as leaves of Autumn strewn,
By that most horrid Chieftain slain
To be by loathesome buzzards torn.

No other words he seemed to hear,
But, in the Artic land was formed,
That Chieftain drawing now so near,
And glory great in battle gained.

So we must either run or fight,
And quicker than his words were said,
As turned hare or deer in flight,
When hunter's hounds pursue they fled.

In order to paliate their conduct for running away in this disgraceful manner, they magnified the forces of the abolitionists beyond that of the report of their scouts and the fear of the Chieftain and his army became deeper and more wide spread throughout Missouri than ever. Had Atchison desired reinforcements, to return to the conflict, it would have been utterly impossible to raise them. They had now lost all confidence in their head as well as the other leaders. The ladies from different parts of Missouri, made and sent to Atchison, quite a number of female under garments, as a fitting testimonial of his conduct on this occasion.

This was the last attempt on the part of the people of Missouri to make Kansas a Slave State by force of arms. The only reliance now of the conspirators was on the administration at Washington, and ballot box stuffing and other frauds in elections, and failing in that they attempted secsssion which ended in the destruction of slavery.

But, on the contrary, since the days of Leonidas and his men whose action, at Thermopylae, has justly been regarded as the glory of the worlds history, there is scarcely anything more truly heroic and grandly sublime than the conduct of the Chieftain and his men from the time they began to collect themselves together at Lawrence until they sat down to breakfast in Atchison's camp, or the camp which Atchison had left. They set out, early in the morning, and made a forced march during the whole day and half the night and after halting a little while by the very first appearance of daylight, they are moving with all possible alacrity into what would seem to all human appearances the very jaws of death. For the enemy consisted of many times there own number. He was in his own selected position and might be fortified and have cannon with which he could rake them at long range, beyond the reach of their guns. He was in numbers sufficient to flank them on each side and, besides, had cavalry sufficient to cut of their retreat or hang on their rear and cut them to pieces, if they should attempt to save themselves by flight. But none of these considerations moved them. Their hearts melt not nor quail not at any possiblities of defeat or death that may be before them. But onward and onward, was their cause; every moment apparrently adding new zeal to their courage; new determination to their purpose and new energy to their movements, as if the

"Soul that is still marching on" inspired every fibre of their being in the early twilight of that morning. Such conduct it seems, should call forth the admiration of angels as well as men. May not the lives of those men, in the sight of heaven, have been considered too precious to be offered up as a sacri-

The Grim Chieftain 113

fice to the Moloch of slavery and that, that was the reason why their numbers were so mysteriously multiplied in the eyes of the enemy so that he was filled with fear and could not stand before them. These men were the rock of Kansas on which slavery was broken and never recovered, but maddened and crazed by the shock, finally, after going through the most horrible death struggles and thoes of agony, sickened and died at Appomattox court house and there was buried in the last ditch.

"No grander or sublime theme,
Was e'er by painters painted, or by
    Poets flung."

Than this short, brilliant, decisive and successful campaign, glorious in its inception; glorious in its execution, and most glorious in its results. On it the freedom of Kansas and the stability of our free institutions and the Republic itself was staked, and most nobly were they defended. When this little campaign is properly written by the unbiased and impartial historian, it will form one of the brightest chapters in the history of Kansas or the world. The people of Kansas, or of Lawrence and Douglas county, to whom the greater share of the land belongs, should in some way erect a monument to the memory of those men and inscribe thereon the names of each and place on the top of it a statue of the Chieftain clad in his old seal skin coat, in which he made his first speech to the free-statemen of Lawrence and declared himself a crusader for freedom while his life should last.

Some attribute the success of this campaign to what they are pleased to call a lucky accident, the mistake as to the number of his men. The answer to this is that the means used were such as would commend success on almost any field of action, and create the circumstances that made the accident, as they term it, possible.

Others say that the Chieftain was playing bluff and that if Atchison had not run he would, but neither the facts, circumstances of the case nor common sense support this view. Others say, that it was merely providential. An over ruling or superintending providence in all the affairs of men is freely conceded, but this must be considered a clear case of providence helping those who help themselves. All attempts to rob these men of the honor that justly belongs to them is fiendish.

The writer regrets that he can not give their names, many of whom, lie the martyrs of freedom, in far distant battlefields. He thinks there could be no more interesting reading than a catalogue of the names, occupation and place of residence of those who yet live and the company and regiment and last resting place of those who are dead.

This campaign was the crowning glory of the Chieftain's career and placed him on the top of the temple of fame in Kansas along side of Charles Robinson. There were now apparently two classes in Rome (or Kansas.) Such conduct would call forth the admiration and command the political support of any people of any age or country, as well as Kansas.

END OF THE BOGUS WARRANTS.

During the administration of Governor Greary, the attempt to punish free-state men for violations of the bogus code, and resistance to what the President was pleased to call the properly constituted authorities of the territory, was abandoned. Whether this course was in obedience to instructions from Washington or in pursuance of some act of amnesty by the bogus legislature, was not generally known. Instructions from Washington to the officials were seldom made public, and few people knew or cared what was done by the law makers at Lecompton. It was ruled, however, that, in order to clear the docket, the parties must come into court and answer or plead to the indictments and when they had done so the cases would be dismissed.

Why such a ruling should be made, was a mystery. Was it done to make court fees and costs? Or was it done to extort, in this way a seeming acknowledgment of the validity of the laws under which the indictments were found and thus let the president and his advisers "Down easy"? The latter was the view generally taken by the parties against whom the indictments were found and they would neither accept service and agree to appear at Lecompton and answer, nor submit to arrest. Warrants for the arrest of Colonel Montgomery and quite a large number of others were placed in the hands of a deputy Marshal, who proceeded to what was then called Southern Kansas to bring the parties into court. Colonel Montgomery treated the marshal, when he called and made known the nature of his visit, very kindly. "I see," said the Colonel, "that you have quite a number of these papers. Will you please let me look over them that I may see the names of those who are to be arrested with me." "Certainly," said the marshal, at the same time handing over the package. After examining them, the Colonel said, "My dear sir, it is very dangerous for you to carry these things around this country, so I will just relieve you of any further responsibility with regard to them and keep them myself. What return the deputy marshal made to the court is not known. Those warrants were never served.

Warrants were also placed in the hands of deputy marshal Arms, among which was one for Colonel John Ritchie, of Topeka. To Colonel Ritchie, the bogus code was the concentrated essence of all political villianies, without the sanction of even the form of law: and any one who should attempt to deprive him of his liberty or property by means of any process by virtue of this code, he regarded a tresspass to be resisted to the death if necessary.

Marshal Arms requested Captains Thompson and Hill, of Topeka, two men of great nerve and courage to go with him to make the arrest, but they answered: "You had better let that job out." The marshal then proceeded alone to Mr. Ritchie's residence, to make the arrest, but was shot through the neck and brought away a corpse. The grand jury failed to find a bill against the Colonel and this was the last attempt made to clear the docket of these cases, by bringing the parties into court to answer. Some other way was found, unless they remain there yet. The Chieftain, having now nothing to fear, and no military or political duties to require his attention, removes his wife and devoted his attention in company with "Jimmy Christian" to the practice of law in the city of Lawrence. But as the profession was largely over stocked and the country new and the people poor and but little for lawyers to do, if he succeeded, once in a while, in catching a client and "skinning him of the hide" amounted to but little. He neither added to his fame nor his fortune by his legal efforts though, it was claimed for him that his skill in gathering in his few and scanty fees was creditable to the profession.

His real or feigned domestic trouble, the terrifleinfilading the Democrats had just given him and the failure of the Republicans of the country to uphold him, and nothing to keep him prominently before the people caused him to feel that his "boom was not booming" but on the decline and he sought an election, and was elected a member of the Leavenworth constitutional convention and asked to be made president of the convention when it assembled at Mineola. This he said would be an endorsement of his past political career by the people of Kansas and place him prominently before the country, and would give the lie to Senator Douglas and others who declared that he was a disgrace to the abolition or free-state party and that they were ashamed of him. To this Martin F. Conway, who desired the position of president to advance his congressional aspirations strongly objected, claiming, it was not right that one man should monopolise all the honors of the party, but finally said that if the Chieftain would resign in his favor, as soon as the convention was organized, that he would yield his objections. Accordingly the Chieftain was chosen, and when the convention assembled at Leavenworth, after adjournment from Mineola, he called it to order and thanking the members for the great honor which they had unanimously confered upon him, in choosing him to preside over their deliberations, said that he much prefered a position on the floor of the convention, that he would feel more at home there, and unconditionally resigned in favor of Martin F. Conway. Thus he appeared, not only, as declining honors that had been heaped upon himself, but as dictating upon whom they should be confered. Nothing noteworthy, in his career, occurred during the convention.

On all questions, he seemed to act with and favor the Conservative wing, that is, those who were in favor of excluding the Negroes entirely and making Kansas a free white state; but at the close of the convention, in a speech he declared most positively, that he belonged to the Radical wing of the free-state party. The Radical wing were largely in the majority.

In this convention, as in nearly all others of a similar kind the members took it upon themselves to arrange who should hold the different state and other offices, when they named there own members for the different positions, and create an office for the special benefit of a member, they did nothing unusual. In the Wyandotte convention, afterwards, judicial districts were formed to suit the aspirations of certain ones.

The slate of the Leavenworth convention for the principal offices, was

 For United States Senators,
THE GOVERNOR,
THE CHIEFTAIN.
 For Congress,
MARTIN F. CONWAY.
 For Governor,
HENRY J. ADAMS.
 For Lieutenant Governor,
J. M. WINCHEL.
 For Chief Justice,
THOMAS EWING, Jr.
 For Superintendent Public Instruction,
ALPHABET ARNY.

As the slate, at the nominating convention, shared the fate of many others of simular kind, the rest of the names are omitted. All the names on the slate were members except the governor's.

The Governor was represented by the members as the first choice and the Chieftain, as the second choice, for the United States Senate. The people considered these positions were due them for the services they had rendered. The Governor's name was not considered for any other position, all considering that he was worthy and deserving of the most honorable place in the gift of the people and that the Chieftain had honestly earned a like position.

But it soon began to be noised abroad throughout the length and breadth of the land that the two men whom the people delighted to honor above all others, were disputing and quarreling by the way, on the old questions, "who should be the greatest" in the kingdom about to be set up, and that each wished to cast the other out into utter darkness and not let him have any place in the new kingdom, but have all the honors unto himself, that his name alone might be great among the people and that he might exercise dominion over them. This was very grevious with the people and did vex them sorely and caused them to talk much one with another and say, "This thing must not surely happen, for we owe both these men great honor and respect for what they have done for us, and it is meat that we should render unto each the honor that is due."

And when the people did learn that, they were waxing exceedingly wroth and hot towards each other, they sent their chief men and men of understanding to them, who should say unto them; 'Not to act thus wickedly like unto foolish men, but to be reconciled one to the other; and that each should receive the honor that was due unto him, but if they continued to act thus wickedly and foolishly, it would bring dissensions, among the people; some saying "I am for the governor" and some saying "I am for the Chieftain" and that great evil instead of good would befall the land." Where they gave no heed unto what was said unto them, the people said: "Albeit, these men will not hearken unto us and hear our voice, nor cease to act like them heathens do, yet we will honor them, nevertheless and give unto each the honor that is due him, then we will be blameless, but one shall not cast the other out and take unto himself all the honor."

To venture an opinion as to the origin of this quarrel, would be useless. That there could not be two Cæsars at the same time, proved true of Kansas, as well as

The Grim Chieftain

of Rome. Many and various efforts were made to put a stop to this silly proceeding on the part of those men it was said, that the people of Lawrence tried to get them to stand in the same stall while General Deitzler, who was a friend to each would strike them down but they could not. During the convention to nominate state officers under the Leavenworth constitution, a number of delegates, prepared a resolution for adoption, declaring that the Governor and the Chieftain were the first and only choice of the people of Kansas, when the proper time came, for United States Senators and offered in the convention for adoption, the delegates who prepared it, were friendly to both the men and thought this course would end the trouble. But the Governor, who was a member of the convention, in an able speech, gave many very good reasons, why the resolution should not be adopted. That the convention was not held for the purpose of declaring who should be United States Senators. but to nominate candidates for state officers. That, if adopted, it would have no binding force, as the convention would be transcending its authority. That the proper. place for instructions of this sort was when nominations for the members of the legislature were made. That the proceeding proposed was unusual. That there was little probability that Kansas would be admitted under the Leavenworth constitution or during the present adminstration and the resolution, if adopted, might be embarrasing hereafter; That the best plan was to let the subject of the choice for senators alone till the proper time came.

The resolution was withdrawn, but the members of the convention throught that the Governor had not given his true reasons for opposing it, and their determination to stand was stronger than ever. The fight continued. Each had a foreman worthy of his steel. The Governor was in no danger, however, he was fighting to save his political standing, or to secure a position. Any position that he desired, such was his hold on the affections of the people, was sure. He was, therefore, regarded as the aggressor, while the Chieftain was looked on, as fighting to save himself.

THE LECOMPTON CONSTITUTION.

The last hope of slavery, was the legitimate offspring of the "Bogus Code," brought forth by Candle Box Calhoun, surveyor general and political hiss of the administration, democracy, and submitted for ratification in the true Lecompton style. The people could vote for it, with or without slavery, but in either case Kansas would be a slave state. The life of this most precious Democratic bantling could not be jeopardized by allowing the people to vote against it. After it had passed through the force of a ratification, in which the free-state men took no part, it was carefully sealed up and entrusted to a special messenger to be carried to Washington and delivered into the hands of the president of the United States. This messenger chanced to be a very particular friend of Senator Stephen A. Douglass, of Illinois. Senator Douglass had now become disgusted and tired of doing the dirty work of the slave power for nothing but promises, which were never redeemed and resolved to play the squatter sovereign clause of the organic act of Kansas for all it was worth, to make himself solid with the northern democracy and people. Learning that his friend the messenger was on his way to Washington, with his precious treasure, Douglass called on him as soon as he arrived and asked to see the sacred parchment before it was delivered to the president. The messenger replied that he could not let him see it, that it was carefully sealed up and his instructions were to deliver it into the hands of the president and let no one see it.

Senator Douglass felt chagrined at being thus snubbed and retorted; "I did not think, after all I have done for you, that you would serve me so." The messenger relented and it was arranged that Senator Douglass should take the constitution and return it at four o'clock P. M. The messenger called on the president and told him that he had just arrived but his trunk, which contained the constitution had not yet come to the hotel, and that he was very tired traveling night and day, and must have some rest, and that he would bring the constitution over at five o'clock or the next morning at such a time as would suit his convenience. "By all means" said the president, "bring it this afternoon, you will have rested sufficiently by that time."

Senator Douglass set clerks to work to making a copy of this quintessence of political villiany. He and the messenger spent the day in talking over their boyhood scenes and the political situation

The Grim Chieftain

in Kansas, until the appointed time to meet the president. The president during the day sent invitations to Senators Slidel, Mason, Benjamin and several others of the high priests, of slavery, to be present at five o'clock P. M., when the long desired culmination of democratic statesmenship was to be received. When the messenger delivered his charge to the president he said: "let me advise the president to his hands of this thing, for it never can be the constitution of Kansas." Whereupon Senator Slidel soundly rebuked him for his impertinence in presuming to advise the president of the United States as to his official duty, when he was only a messenger. (Exit Messenger.)

With this contemptible swindle, the president transmitted a special message to congress recommending the admission of Kansas as a state under it, but Senator Douglass was fully prepared and in an able speech showed up all the vileness, of this attempt to rob the people of Kansas of their political rights in a manner that all the powers of the president with all his patronage, backed by the slave power, could not force it through congress. And, when the people of Kansas got an opportunity to vote against it when it was returned for re-ratification, they will burry it so deep that Gabriels trumpet will never awake it. Thus ended the attempt to force slavery into Kansas and subvert the government of the United States into a slaveholding oligarchy. The slaveholders, now, turned there attention again to secession and rebellion, as they had done before. A particular friend of Jefferson

Davis then secretary of war, in the winter of 1855. 1856 visited Fort Larimie in Nebraska and got the names of all the army officers who would cast their fortunes with the south in case of secession and war. Had Fremont been elected, rebellion would have followed.

THE KILLING OF CAPTAIN JENKINS.

The people having now secured control of their own political affairs, everybody was happy and so was the Chieftain. The time when he should receive the long sought senatorship was drawing near. But who can tell what a day may bring forth, or what fortune may have in store for him? One morning he arose with hopes and prospects, bright as man could wish. At night those hopes and prospects were sunk in the gloom of darkness seemingly never to rise again. In the morning all were ready to bestow on him the highest honors in the state, but with the setting sun all men had forsaken him. He had shot and killed Captain Jenkins, of Lawrence, and stood raigned before the court of his country as a manslayer. The news flys. Every moment adds new pinions to its wings and new vigor to its flight. Men formed their judgment from what they first heard, not waiting for the evidence to mitigate or justify it. And when it was proven on the trial, that, only, after using all prudent and proper means to avoid a conflict he was compelled, in self defense in order to save his own life, to shoot his assailant, but few ever saw the evidence and fewer read it. They did not know but that he had been acquitted by some technicality or defect of the law. They knew he had killed a man, but did not know that he was justified in doing so. They felt that he had forfeited all claim to their political support. Some claimed that the enemies of the Chieftain got Captain Jenkins, who was a brave and fearless man, under the influence of liquor and urged him to make the attack, knowing that in the conflict one or the other would be killed, or that Jenkins would drive the Chieftain from the land in dispute. If the Chieftain should get killed that would be the end of him; if he should kill Jenkins, that would work his political ruin, or downfall, or if Jenkins should drive him from his claim, he would be stigmatized, as a coward, and be out of the way. The writer never heard any evidence to substantiate this horrid claim and could not believe it without the best of proof.

On a former occasion when his political barque was dashed to pieces, he found relief in denouncing the authors of his misery and in meditating revenge; but even that solace is denied him, for Jenkins is in his grave. All was darkness and many others rose up to contend for his place, and men ceased even to notice him, as they passed him by. Nor was he even a laughing stock for his enemy, who would have scorned to add to his humiliation, had it been possible so to do.

Care worn, haggard, reduced almost to a skeleton, the picture of dispair, clad in the old seal skin coat, the writer met him in Lawrence one day, and extending the hand in a familar way, said "How" after the manner of an Indian. After the salutations were passed, the Chieftain said to the writer, that he had been wanting to see him for some time, to have a talk with him on a matter of great importance, and asked the writer to go and take dinner with him. The writer did not wish to have any conversation with him fearing that he would wish him to join in an attempt for his political resurrection, yet he could not find it in his heart to refuse the inviatation. During the walk to his old home little or nothing was said by either. The writer dreading the conversation, and wondering why the Chieftain did not begin it and studying also, what answer to make; and the Chieftain probably, diverting his mind, did not think proper to say anything. A thought occurred to the writer, that probably there would be some others at his house one of his confidential little caucuses, and that he did not wish to open up the subject until the company was reached. Arriving at his house, however, there was nobody there but his wife, who scarcely noticed the writer and as women, sometimes, do when their husbands bring in a stranger unawares for dinner, appeared to be in a bad humor or sulky. She looked almost as careworn and distressed as the Chieftain and no doubt was in as much trouble. What money she may have got, was all gone. The trial and other expenses were great and nothing was left to keep the wolf from her door. That despondency and gloom were pictured in her countenance is not surprising. Placing her scanty dinner on the table she took a seat by a window to look out, leaving the Chieftain to pour out the coffee and wait on the table. Little was said during dinner and little on the way back to Massachusetts street. The writer attempted to say something, several times, careful, however, to avoid the great subject on which he had supposed his companion desired to talk, but there was little or no response. Probably the writer did not do right, but he did not feel like joining in what seemed, at the time, to be an impossible undertaking.

CHAPTER V.

The fourth of July 1869, he speaks at Auburn How he gets the inviatation.

The fourth of July was approaching and as the year of jubilee had now fully come in Kansas, the people every where throughout the territory were making unusual preparations to celebrate the day in a manner befitting the occasion. All the prominent speakers were engaged to hold forth in the various towns and cities, but the Chieftain remained without an inviatation to glorify the bird of freedom on the national anniversary of American Independence, and had it not been for the failure of the little town of Auburn in Shawnee county, to secure a speaker suitable to there notions, would have remained in obsurity for that day, if not forever. Auburn, at that time, an ambitious and enterprising little place, was making extraordinary preparation, for the coming celebration and wished to get a more than ordinary speaker, from abroad, to give eclat to their young city. The committee made several attempts for this purpose and failed. All the speakers to whom they applied, having been previously engaged by the large towns or cities. The committee then tried to utilize "home talent" and secure one of the several men in the neighborhood, who were capable of making a very fair address but the time was so short they found this a very difficult matter, if not impossible, while the negotiations of the committee were in progress, two citizens of Auburn went to Lawrence on some business and happened to meet the Chieftain and learning that he was not engaged, took the responsibility upon themselves to ask him to come to Auburn and blow off any pent up patriotism that might be in his bosom. They explained to him the situation but told him they thought it would be all right. He accepted the inviatation without any hesitation whatever, saying that he would come and if not all right, he would spend the day there and listen to some one else, whoever he might be.